Loneliness

by Laurie Beckelman

Series Consultant
John Livingstone, M.D.

Crestwood House
New York

Maxwell Macmillan Canada
Toronto

Maxwell Macmillan International
New York   Oxford   Singapore   Sydney

For Jason,
with hope that he learns to transform
growing pains into growth

Author's Note:
Many teenagers generously shared their thoughts and experiences with me.
The quotes in this book are based on their stories.

Crestwood House
Macmillan Publishing Company
866 Third Avenue, New York, NY 10022

Maxwell Macmillan Canada, Inc.
1200 Eglinton Avenue East, Suite 200
Don Mills, Ontario M3C 3N1

Macmillan Publishing Company is part of the
Maxwell Communication Group of Companies.

First Edition
Design: Lynda Fishbourne, Hemenway Design Associates
Packaging: Prentice Associates Inc.
Photos:
Superstock: Cover, 4, 30, 36, PhotoEdit: (Myrleen Ferguson) 10, 22, 27, 41, 45,
(Tony Freeman) 18, 29, 38,(Richard Hutchings) 14, 20, (David Young-Wolff) 33

Printed in the United States of America
10 9 8 7 6 5 4 3 2 1

Library of Congress Cataloging-in-Publication Data
Beckelman, Laurie.
Loneliness / by Laurie Beckelman — 1st ed.
p. cm.— (Hot line)
Includes bibliographical references and index.
ISBN 0-89686-843-5   0-382-24745-0 (pbk.)
1. Loneliness—Juvenile literature. [1. Loneliness.] I. Title. II. Series.
BF575.L7B43 1994
158'.2—dc20   93-5625

Summary: A discussion of loneliness, an emotion common in teenagers. Provides a
definition of loneliness, explains frequent causes, and offers suggestions for coping with it.

HOT LINE

Loneliness

CONTENTS

I can be

partying,

you know,

listening to

some new

CDs or

shooting

hoops, when

suddenly

I feel like . . .

I don't know.

Like I'm

someone

else in a

different

skin.

The Voices of Loneliness

Listen to the voices of loneliness:

Sherri: I'm, like, standing there, holding my tray, looking out at the cafeteria. I don't know where to sit. I want to sit with Tara. But she's with Jenny and Marie. And I'm afraid they'll, like, ignore me. Then Jimmy, this geek, sticks his elbow in my side and says, "Sherri has no frie-ends." I died. And he saw it, too. He went off laughing to sit with some moron friend. And I just stood there. He was right. I have no friends.

Michael: I hang with this really cool crowd. I mean, we are *it* in my school. So why should I feel lonely, right? But I can be partying, you know, listening to some new CDs or shooting hoops, when suddenly I feel like . . . I don't know. Like I'm someone else in a different skin. It's like I have all this stuff inside . . . doubts . . . questions . . . But if I say anything, man, they'd laugh me down. I mean, I'm Mr. C, right? Mis-ter Cool. So I just party harder. No one knows how I feel.

Melissa: Paul was away all summer. He didn't write. I couldn't wait 'til he got back. But when he did, he wouldn't even talk to me. Before the summer, we'd been . . . well, you know. And then he didn't write? And when he came home, he wouldn't *talk* to me? Oh, God. It was the worst. I never felt so alone.

Jon: It's always the same. I get home, throw my stuff in my room, grab a Coke. Then nothing. I stand in the kitchen and I hear these sounds—the refrigerator, water dripping. Even the clock makes a sound, a tiny electric hum. I hate it, so I turn on the tube. Then I wait for someone to come home.

Sherri, Michael, Melissa, and Jon are kids like you. Like you, they know **loneliness**. Everyone does. Loneliness is the feeling of being cut off or separate from others. It is a normal feeling we experience on and off throughout life. It may come for many reasons. Loneliness visits as we wait for the phone to ring. It greets us when we enter an empty house; it roars above the screams of our parents' fights. The feeling comes unexpectedly in the middle of a party, making strangers out of friends.

Loneliness sinks its claws when we sit alone on a Saturday night or when we're picked last for the basketball team. It can stare back at us from the mirror. We feel trapped in changing bodies and are confused by moods that shift with lightning speed. We are like strangers to ourselves.

Loneliness can feel awful. It can yell at us: You don't belong. No one loves you. You're alone. No one cares. No one understands.

But loneliness also has a gentler, hopeful voice. It is the voice of growth and change. If we listen carefully, we can hear it asking questions: Why do you sometimes feel alone even when you're with your friends? Could you fill those hours after school with something you enjoy more than TV? Would it help if you told someone how you feel?

This gentle voice can help us. It can challenge us to examine our needs and to better understand ourselves. It can help us grow.

This book is about listening to the voices of loneliness. It is about the relationships we need and why they sometimes fail us. But most of all, it is about understanding loneliness so that we can use it as a tool for growth.

People Who Need People

For Adam, loneliness is a "black, empty feeling." Melissa says it "feels like someone's grabbing my heart and squeezing hard." Adam says he feels most lonely when he can't find friends to play street hockey on a Saturday afternoon. Melissa felt that her heart was squeezed so tight it would burst after Paul, her boyfriend, wouldn't talk to her.

For Chris, loneliness is "like being trapped in a space bubble. You can't touch anyone and no one can touch you." He says he sometimes feels this way when he's out with his family. "It's weird. I know they're trying. But I feel like we're on separate planets. They just don't understand."

Adam feels lonely because he can't find friends. Melissa experiences loneliness because she lost her boyfriend. Chris feels it because he can't connect with his family. As different as these stories are, they have one thing in common: Adam, Melissa, and Chris all feel cut off from relationships that matter to them.

This is the heart of loneliness: Why you feel it depends on who *you* are and the relationships *you* need. You might have 1 friend or 20. You might have a large family or live alone with one parent, grandparent, or aunt. You might belong to half the clubs in school or spend your afternoons alone watching TV. You might have a date every Saturday night or never go out. It doesn't matter. What matters is how you *feel* about your relationships. If you feel understood and cared for, you probably don't feel lonely. But if you feel cut off, you may experience the black emptiness. The squeezed heart. The isolation of a space bubble. We all feel this way sometimes. If we understand why, we can hear the hopeful voice of loneliness rather than the blaming one. This understanding can help us feel better even if we are still lonely.

Our need to connect with others is ever present. Indeed, our survival may depend on it. Infants who are not touched enough do not grow or develop well, even when they get enough food. Prisoners kept apart from others sometimes lose their minds.

Loneliness may make our bodies less able to fight disease. Many scientists now think that feelings affect the **immune system.** They have found that

If you feel understood and cared for, you probably don't feel lonely. But if you feel cut off, you may experience the black, empty feeling of loneliness.

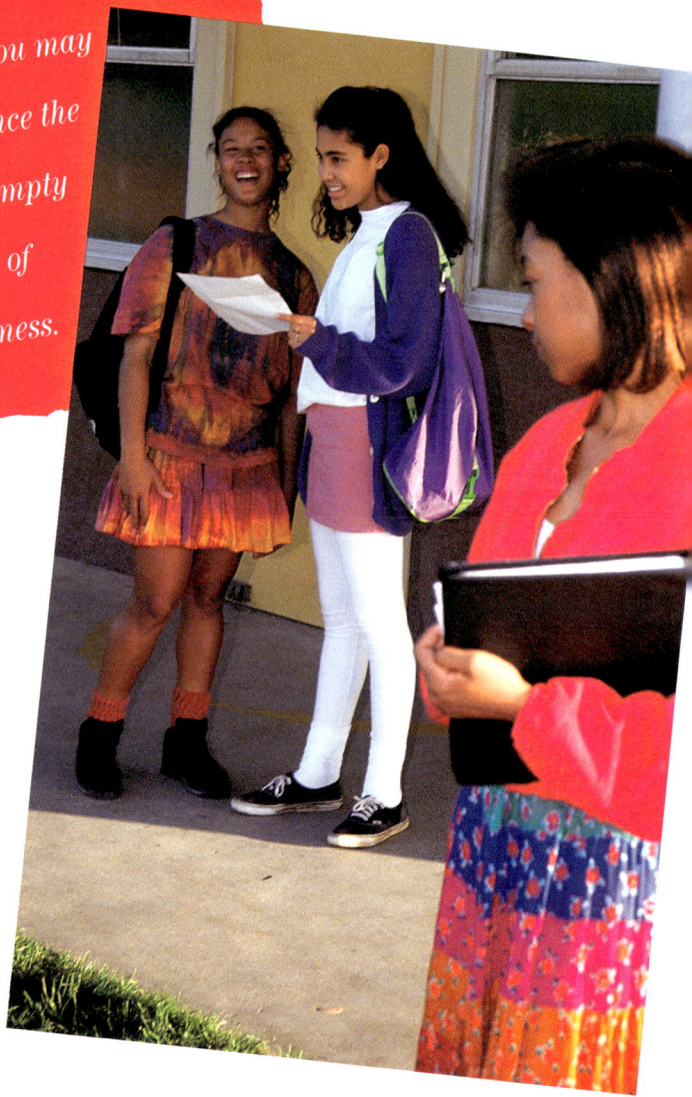

people who feel lonely have lower levels of certain **immune cells.**

Our bodies and minds tell an obvious truth: People need people. From infancy on, we discover ourselves and our world through relationships. Through family, then friends, and, someday, lovers, we learn what we value and what others value in us. Through them we discover new ideas, new interests, new attitudes. We try these on, keeping some for a season and others for life. As we fill out our wardrobe of self-knowledge, we grow and change. And as we change, so do our relationships. This change can bring closeness and connection. But it can also bring loneliness.

The Many Faces of Loneliness

When Paul broke up with her, Melissa couldn't bear it. She felt so lonely, she says, that "I thought I would die."

Robert S. Weiss, the first researcher to offer a **theory** of loneliness, would call what Melissa felt **situational loneliness.** It came from a situation in her life: breaking up with Paul. Moving to a new school, the divorce of one's parents, and fighting with a friend are other situations that can lead to loneliness.

But Gabe felt a different kind of loneliness. A "loner," he was shy, moody, and critical of himself and others. He did not make friends easily. His loneliness came from within. Parts of his personality and his feelings about himself kept him from reaching out to others. He *could* make friends; it was just hard. He had to work to believe in himself and to trust that others would like him.

Researchers Noreen E. Mahon and Adela Yarcheski wondered whether most teen loneliness was like Melissa's or like Gabe's. In a study of 112 students, they found that Melissa was much more typical than Gabe.

This is good news, because the loneliness Melissa felt is more likely to be **transient**: It passes quickly. This happened for Melissa. In a few weeks the hand of loneliness loosened its grip on her heart. She adjusted to being without Paul and started dating other guys.

When someone does not adjust well to a change in his or her life, **chronic loneliness** can occur. This is loneliness that lasts at least two years. Meg's mother died when Meg was nine. Shortly after, Meg and her father moved to be near an aunt who could watch Meg after school. But Meg never felt close to her aunt and never made friends at the new school. She spent many afternoons in her room, looking at pictures of her mother and crying.

"I was so lonely for my mom. All I wanted to do was join her," says Meg. Her loneliness did not pass until she saw a counselor who helped her accept her loss. One thing that helped Meg was to join a group of kids who had also lost a parent. "I finally had people who understood—*really* understood," she says.

Being part of a group can help tame lonely feelings. In fact, researchers believe that people can be close to family and friends and still feel lonely if they don't have

We can create a sense of community. Being part of a group of friends at school, or belonging to a club, a team, a religious organization, or a neighborhood group is one way.

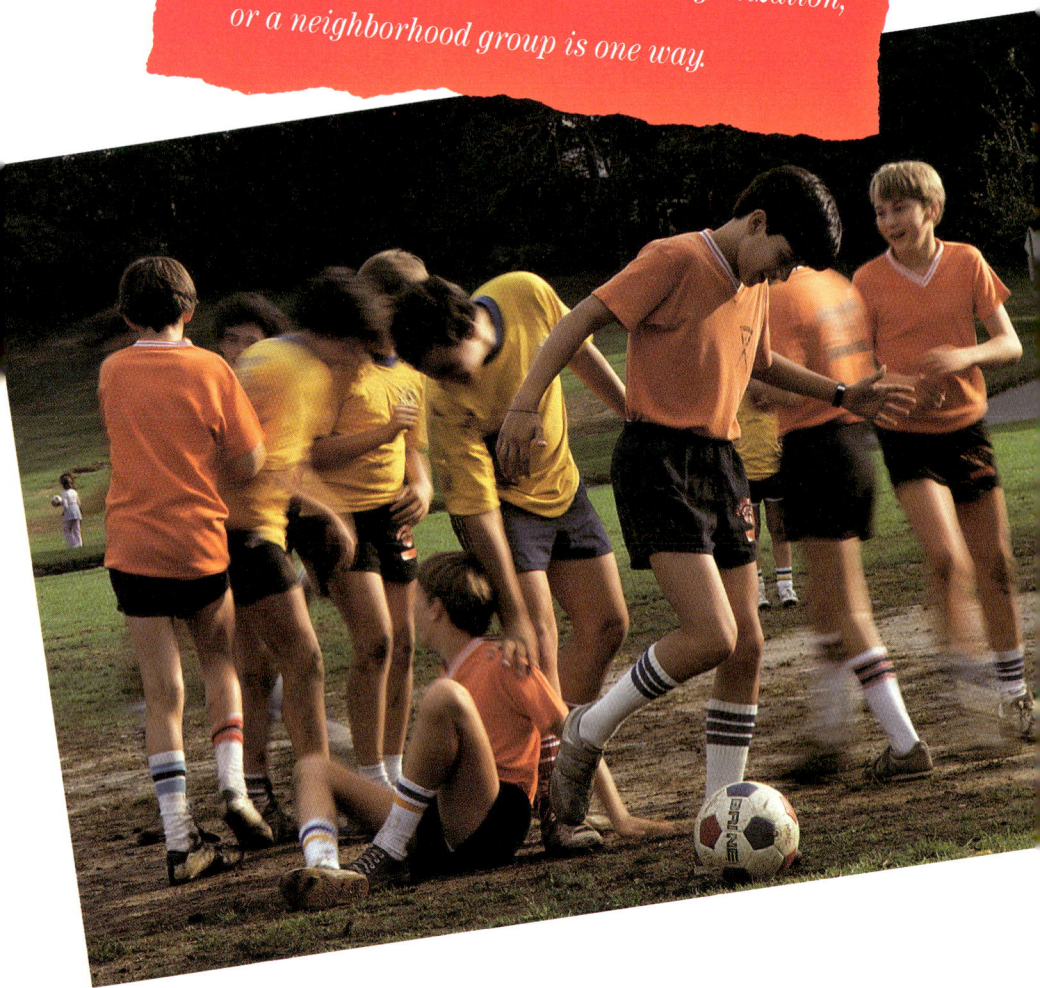

a sense of **community,** of belonging to a larger group.

Some believe that today's **culture** makes finding community hard. In the past, most people married within their ethnic or religious group. They raised their families in the community in which they had grown up. If teenagers skipped school and headed for the local diner, their parents would probably hear about it. If the waitress didn't know the families, the banker, the butcher, or the baker the teenagers passed along the way most likely would!

But today the average American will move 12 times. We may hardly know our neighbors, and we no longer need the banker, the butcher, or the baker. We get our money from teller machines. We buy our food pre-packaged. With faxes and computers, we don't even need to talk!

What's more, our culture prizes independence over community. Clichés such as "everyone for himself (or herself)" show our bias. So do our **myths,** the stories that tell who we are as a culture. They feature the lone rider on the plains, the lone pioneer family taming the wilderness, the lone immigrant come to make it in a new land. Our TV and comic book heroes take independence one step further: From the Lone Ranger to Batman, they wear masks to hide their identity.

The myth of **self-sufficiency** can make us unaware of our need for community. We pay for the freedom we gain with **alienation**. Fortunately, we can create a sense of community. Being part of a group of friends at school, or belonging to a club, a team, a religious organization, or a neighborhood group is one way.

Perhaps you have read this chapter and thought: But what about me? I have friends. I'm part of a group. But I *still* feel lonely. Don't panic. Sometimes loneliness comes and goes for no apparent reason. No event triggers it—no lack of closeness with friends or family or community. This feeling is so common in adolescence that **psychiatrist** John Livingstone coined the term **developmental loneliness:** loneliness that comes and goes during the teen years. This loneliness results from the normal changes that take place during adolescence. Reaching out to friends and family can sometimes lessen the lonely feelings. Understanding why the feelings occur can help us accept them more easily.

The Loneliest Age

Sherri: It was supposed to be a real special day, right? Like, my mom was taking me shopping and for lunch. But I was so bummed. I just had this really big fight with Tara, my best friend, because, like, she hates my other friends and won't even say hello when I'm with them. And, like, I couldn't talk about it. I don't know why. I used to tell my mom everything. But now . . . I don't know. It's different. So I didn't talk. I mean, not at all! I could tell it hurt my mom. But I couldn't help it. I kept thinking, "I'm losing everyone," you know? Tara. My mom. It was the pits.

Michael: I hope this doesn't sound crazy, but sometimes I lie in bed just thinking. You know, trying to figure out what it's all about. I mean, man, what is it all about? Anyway, I guess it worries my dad, 'cause the other day he sat me down for a talk.

You know, he said how I was spending too much time in my room, doing nothing, blah, blah, blah. I just went, "Uh-huh," "Yeah," "Right, Dad," but I thought, "Man, didn't you ever feel this way? Am I the only one?"

Who am I?
What is my place
in the world?
Will I, can I,
make it?

The confusion and separateness Sherri and Michael feel are not only normal—they're common. At no time in our lives do our relationships change more than in our teens. They change because we change, not only in our bodies but also in our hearts and minds. Along with fuller breasts or the first hint of a beard comes a new need for intimacy with people outside the family. Along with a deeper voice or broader hips comes a greater ability to think. We can ask "what if," imagine the future, and puzzle through a problem in ways children simply cannot.

Our changing hearts and minds cause us to see old relationships in new ways. Perhaps the dance teacher we once adored now seems old-fashioned; our weekly dinners with Dad have become a drag. We would rather talk on the phone with a friend than go shopping with Mom. We would rather find a date for Saturday night than hang out with the guys.

Adolescence is a time of self-discovery. In our teens, we forge the sense of self that will guide us to satisfying love and work in adulthood. To do this, we must question, imagine, dream about the future. Like Michael, we might spend time just thinking, asking life's big questions: Who am I? What is my place in the world? Will I, can I, make it?

These are lonely questions because no one can answer them for us. What's more, to find answers, we

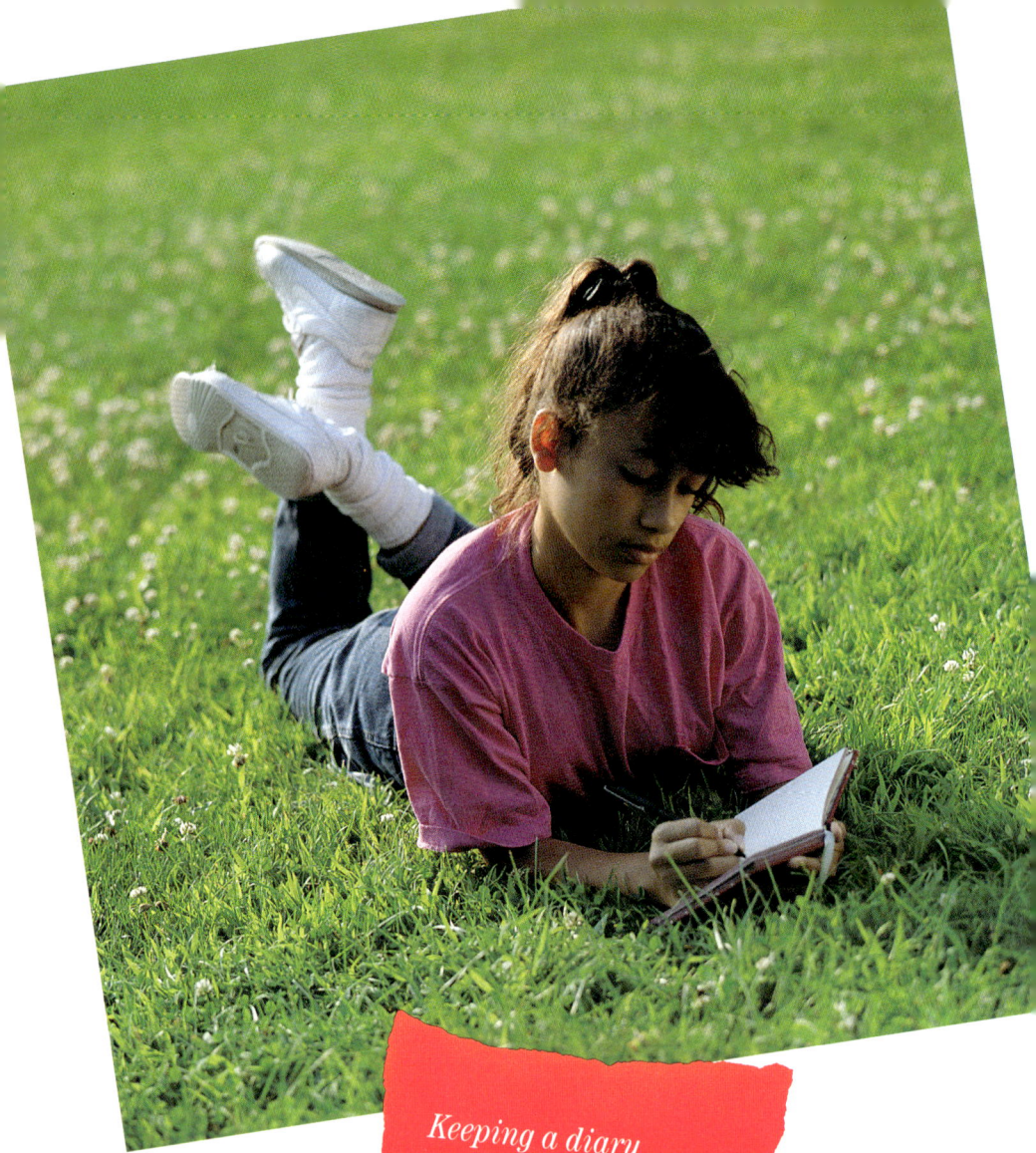

Keeping a diary
or recording our
thoughts with a tape
recorder can help us
explore our needs.

must test the values and ideas of our childhoods. We break away from our pasts. But we do not yet see our futures. This produces loneliness. It may be why studies find that teens are the loneliest Americans.

But these lonely questions can lead us to a greater sense of belonging: They help us know ourselves. As we find out who we are and what we can be in the world, we also discover what we like and need in other people. This can help us understand why some of our relationships seem empty and others satisfying. Keeping a diary or recording our thoughts with a tape recorder can help us explore our needs. So can taking classes or joining groups that let us test new talents. Trusting that we will find answers to the questions helps, too. As we discover what is most important to us, we become more confident in who we are and more comfortable in our relationships.

As children,
we rely on our
parents or
other close
adults
for just about
everything.
But in our
teens we must
separate from
those who
care for us, in
order to find
ourselves.

Home Is Where the Heart Is

"**I** wish my parents trusted me more," says Diana. "I mean, I can't even be late walking home from school with a friend without my mother freaking. But then, sometimes, I wish it were more like it used to be, when they used to check my homework and stuff."

Much of the loneliness teens report comes from changing relationships at home. We first learn what it is to love and be loved from our parents or others who care for us. From these first attachments we learn that those we love will feed us when we're hungry, laugh with us when we're happy, hold us when we hurt. We learn that we are lovable. We learn that we are safe.

As children, we rely on our parents or other close adults for just about everything. Their beliefs, dreams, and prejudices shape our own. We need this structure and guidance. It is the springboard from which we dive into adolescence.

And dive we must. We must leave the safe harbor of our parents' love to explore the waters of our own longings, to discover who we are and what we have to contribute to this world. We must separate from our parents, or others who take care of us, to find ourselves. Yet we still need the safety of their love. These needs are such opposites that they can confuse and anger us. It's hard to feel two different ways at once. But it's okay. People often have conflicting feelings.

The push–pull toward independence is tough for everyone. Parents may not know when to hold on or when to let go. Teens may not, either. Both the adults and the teenagers may be struggling toward a new type of relationship, one that allows independence *and* connection.

This struggle is by nature lonely. Many stresses on today's families make it even worse. Divorce or long work hours mean that some parents simply are not there for their kids. Losing a job or a loved one, being poor or ill, can leave parents too drained to care for their children well. Problems like alcohol or drug abuse can isolate family members from one another.

Says Jon: "Since her divorce, my mom expects me to

be the man of the house. She even tells me that. So I try. I mean, she has to work and stuff now. And she's trying to get her life back together, you know—dating, seeing friends. So I try not to bug her."

Such stresses affect everyone in a family. Too often they pull us apart. We feel too tired, too hurt, too scared to reach out for the love we need. Or to let it in. As a result, we feel lonely. In some families problems like these are ignored. Or worse, they are denied. This denial can leave members feeling even more alone. But even in the worst situations, parents or other trusted adults can be there for us. If we can find the courage to reach out to them, to ask them to listen without judging us, we may be surprised to find that they can.

A Small Circle of Friends

When the world seems to be swimming around you and there seems nowhere to go, a real friend will be there to lead you away from darkness and fear.

Sherri wrote that. "My friends are more important than anyone," she says. Many teens share her feelings. As we pull away from our families, we rely more on our friends. Not having friends, or feeling that we have the wrong friends, can be very lonely. In fact, studies show that most teens name lack of friendship as the reason they feel lonely.

Most of us need different friends for different reasons. We need best friends with whom we can share our deepest selves. We need a crowd that likes and accepts us. We need friends with whom to share special interests. It is not surprising that we feel lonely if we don't have the friends we need.

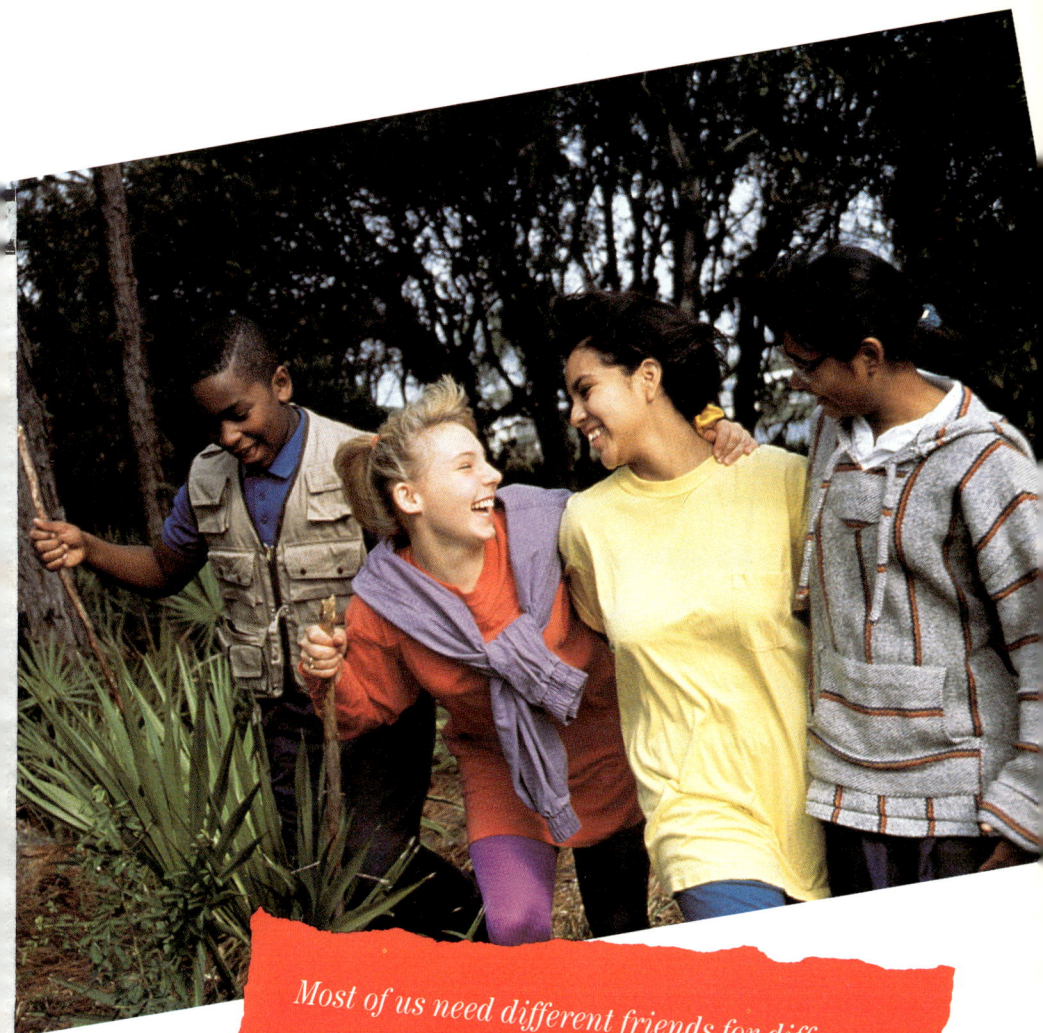

Most of us need different friends for different reasons. We need best friends with whom we can share our deepest selves. We need a crowd that likes and accepts us.

But we can also feel lonely *with* our friends.

Sometimes new interests strain old friendships. Adam and his best friend were crazy about hockey. They'd play hockey, talk hockey, and watch hockey. But Adam found a new interest: acting. "I still love hockey, but that's *all* Kevin ever wants to do or talk about," he says. "If I tell him about my acting, he puts me down. He thinks it's weird." Adam feels different from his friend now. He feels he has to hide an important side of himself. But friends should celebrate their differences and learn from each other.

Belonging to different crowds can strain friendship, too. "My best friend is Tara. At least usually she is," says Sherri. "But, like, the problem is, she's in with all the popular kids in school, and I'm not. So sometimes she ignores me."

Sherri explains that she's too shy to feel comfortable with Tara's other friends. Sometimes she thinks that if only she could be just like Tara, she'd never feel lonely. What she doesn't know is that Tara feels lonely, too.

Being "in with the in crowd" isn't always the key to good friendships. Just ask Michael. "Everyone thinks I'm cool. The hottest kids in school hang at my house. We got us a band set up so we can jam, and my dad's not home 'til seven at night. Usually it's cool. But sometimes . . . I don't know. Sometimes I feel like I'm up on a stage, putting on the happy face for my friends. If they *really* knew me, they'd split."

We shouldn't need to put on a happy face or deny our interests for real friends. We shouldn't need to be other than who we are. Real friends help us feel good about ourselves. They support what's best in us, and we do the same for them. When the friends we have don't fill these roles, we can feel lonely indeed.

We shouldn't need to put on a happy face or deny our interests for real friends. We shouldn't need to be other than who we are.

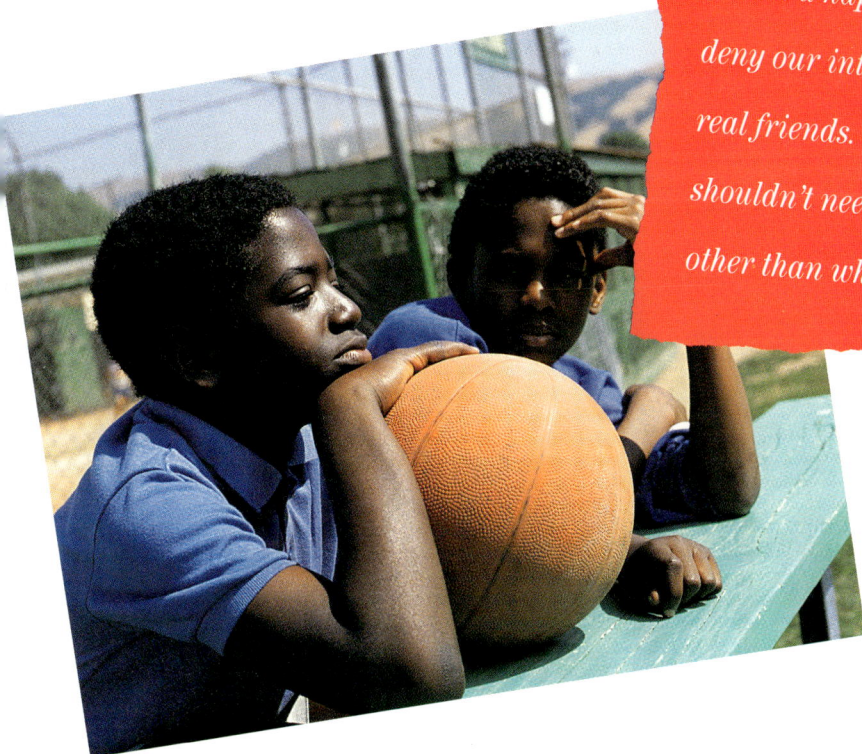

We want to be loved for who we are. So do those we love. This cannot happen until we see each other as we are, not as we wish each other to be.

Sweethearts, Broken Hearts

"**I** used to think, if only I could go with Matt," says Melissa. "He's real tall and dresses great and *everyone* likes him. I thought he was perfect."

Melissa did go with Matt—for a while. But it turned out that his idea of a good time was to hang out with his two best friends, drink beer, and fool around. Melissa found his friends boring. She hated beer but drank to keep him company. Two months into her romance, she was disappointed, lonely, and ready to move on. "I can't believe he turned out to be such a jerk," she says.

Few of us make it through our teens without feeling the pain of a broken heart. We may fall in love with someone who doesn't know we exist. We may give our heart to someone who leaves us two weeks later. The object of our love might like us just as a friend or may disappoint us. Like Melissa, we may fall in love with the way someone looks or with an idea of what he or she is, not with the real person.

Few things feel better than falling in love, but that wonderful sensation may not last. We learn soon enough that the person we love is not a god or goddess but a boy or girl who can hurt as well as please us. We learn that he or she cannot always give us what we want and may want things we cannot give. We learn that we are separate individuals. We learn that being in love cannot make us a satisfied and complete person—we must make ourselves whole.

This discovery can make us feel lonely. But it is also the key to making love last. We want to be loved for who we are. So do those we love. This cannot happen until we see each other as we are, not as we wish each other to be. It can't happen until we learn that we can hold and help and love each other despite our differences. And it cannot happen until we realize that love is not a substitute for **self-development.** Love can help. It can make us feel appreciated and understood. It can support our growth, but it cannot do our growing for us.

Learning to love takes time. And, like riding a bicycle, it takes practice. When we totter in love, we bruise our heart instead of our knees. But the same advice applies: Get up and try again. And don't blame yourself.

In our teens, when these feelings are so new, we may doubt that we'll ever be able to get up and try again. We may think that because we failed at love once, we will always fail. We may feel that we will always be lonely. And the loneliness is intense. Because we share so much more of ourselves with a girlfriend or boyfriend than with other people, we hurt that much more when love fails.

But just as most people learn to ride a bicycle if they try, most of us find love. That doesn't mean that we never feel lonely in a loving relationship. We do. How lonely depends, in part, on what we expect.

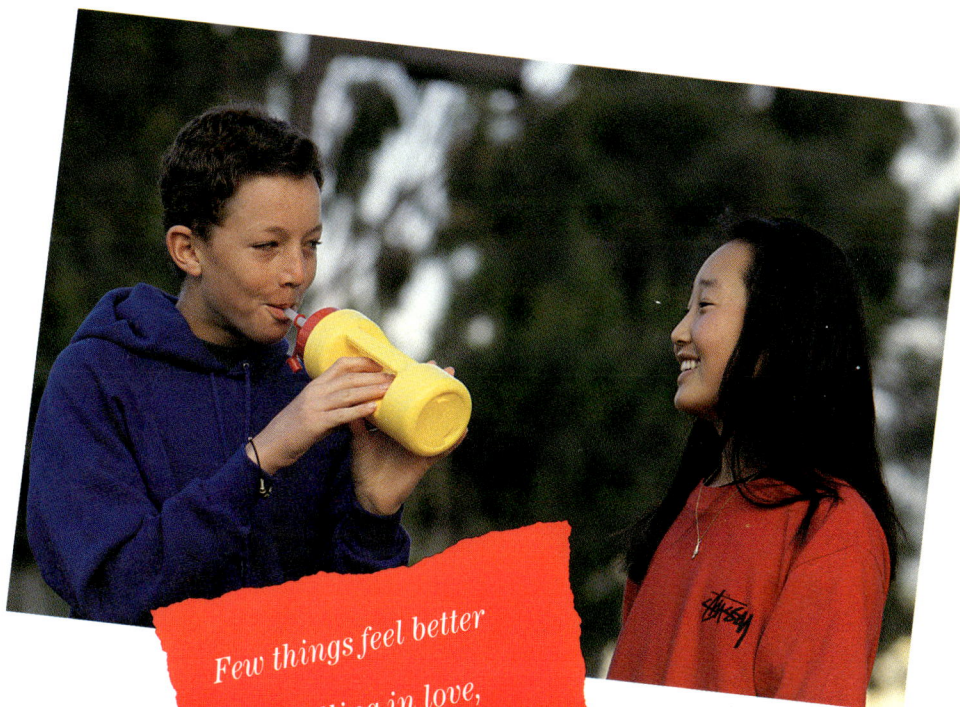

Few things feel better than falling in love, but that wonderful sensation may not last.

Great Expectations

Some critics of modern life say we put too much stress on love as the key to happiness. They feel that we often forget that we need creative work as well as love to know and accept ourselves. Because we ask too much of love, they say, we are often disappointed and lonely.

Some say it's no wonder that we expect too much, not only from boyfriends and girlfriends but also from family and friends. We are flooded with models of perfection. TV families, from the Cleavers to the Huxtables, face crises with closeness, good humor, and insight. In the movies true friends always know the right thing to say. Ads selling everything from cola to jeans promise a world of laughter and love.

On the big screen as well as the small, boy meets girl again and again and again. Nerd gets babe. Babe gets jock. Jock gets brain. No matter how odd the match, love triumphs. And when it does, all problems fade away. Because of the girl's love, the boy accepts his true self. He might be a teen werewolf, an alien duck, or a hairy, fanged beast. It doesn't matter. The girl's love will pull him through.

And what about the girl? The boy's love frees the beauty queen hiding beneath the mousy hair and the old-fashioned glasses. It lets the bookworm dance free. It saves the fast but good-hearted girl from the bad men who prey upon her. It turns the mermaid into a princess.

The problem with these love-saves-all stories is that they can lead us to expect too much. We do need fantasies. We need models of "what could be" to guide us in our struggle for intimacy and growth. But models that are unrealistic can hurt more than they help. They can make the gap between "what could be" and "what is" painfully wide. In this gap, loneliness thrives.

TV and movies often suggest that our relationships will take care of us, when in reality we must take care of them—and of ourselves. They tell us that people who love us will always be there. But in reality, parents may not be able to give us the help we need. Some parents travel on business. Some families are torn apart by divorce. Many parents come home from work so tired that they can't listen to our problems, let alone offer the perfect advice. Some may drink or do drugs. And sometimes parents listen as best they can but still don't understand.

Our friends aren't always there for us, either. They may tell our secrets or elbow in on our dates. They might pressure us to drop an old friend or to try drugs we don't want or sex we're not ready for. They might cut us off when we try to explain how we feel, or they may talk only about themselves. They might disappoint us or bore us even when we know they care.

Our relationships are more like a rutted country road than a smooth superhighway. If we expect the potholes, the disappointments, we can learn to steer around them. But if we expect the superhighway, we might turn off the road before we really get started on our journey. We might run from temporary loneliness only to find a dead end.

TV and movies often suggest that our relationships will take care of us, when in reality we must take care of them—and of ourselves.

Sex, Lies, and Loneliness

For Jon, running from loneliness means turning on "the boob tube," as he calls TV. He's not very interested in the shows he watches, "but at least it fills the time," he says. But once the set is off, nothing in Jon's life has changed.

Melissa runs to boyfriends. "Sometimes I think, if I didn't have a boyfriend, I'd be free. But then I worry that if I stop having one, I won't ever have another one again." The problem is that Melissa's boyfriends never really meet her need to feel loved. "It's always great in the beginning," she says. "You let a guy get close 'cause you need to be loved, but then, when he turns out to be a jerk—ugh!"

For Sherri, running from loneliness takes a different form. "I never want to let my friends down," she says, "because, like, maybe then they won't be my friends. So I do whatever they want, even if I don't want

Hours lost to the oblivion of TV do not make loneliness go away. Neither does overeating, drinking, or taking drugs.

to. I always say, 'Sure, great.' "

Other teens (as well as adults) feed the emptiness inside with ice-cream sundaes and boxes of cookies. Or worse, they mask it with the short-lived pleasure of getting high. Unfortunately, none of these attempts to deal with loneliness work. Sex without love, friendships built on lies, hours lost to the oblivion of TV do not make loneliness go away. Neither does overeating, drinking, or taking drugs. These efforts at escape don't help us understand why we feel lonely or what changes would help us feel better.

Up on the Roof

"**L**oneliness is confusing," says Diana. "You feel lonely, but you don't know who for. You cry but you don't know why."

Diana is right. Loneliness *is* confusing. It can have so many causes that we don't always know why we feel the way we do. Sometimes the feeling comes out of nowhere—we're hit with a teenage loneliness attack that has no cause except adolescence. At other times loneliness is a warning that something is missing in our lives. We need time—quiet time—to listen to the warning, to figure out what it is trying to say. This is why sometimes the best way to deal with loneliness is to choose to be alone for a while and to use the time to discover ourselves.

Henry David Thoreau, a great American writer, chose the solitude of country life over the bustle of the city. His reason? He wrote: "Not till we are lost, in other words, not till we have lost the world, do we begin to find ourselves."

Finding ourselves is the key to understanding our loneliness. Some people find that having a private place helps them sort out their feelings. Sherri goes to a fenced-off brook behind her housing development. For Melissa it isn't a place but a pet that helps. "My cat gets me through the times of loneliness," she says. "I hold her and pet her and think. Then I don't feel so bad."

We may be alone during these times of **reflective solitude,** but we carry in our hearts the people we love and care for. We can call up their images to help us understand our feelings. We can try out a conversation with a parent or a friend. We can write letters that we may never mean to send but that help us clarify our feelings. We can write to a friend who has hurt us, to someone new we'd like to know, to a parent we feel never listens, to someone we admire who could give us advice. We can write the answers to these letters we would like to receive, too. In so doing, we can better understand what we want from the people to whom we've written—and what we need.

When we're alone, we can think about the last time we felt really loved and cared for. We can use the image that comes to mind to help us see what is missing now. We can also use it as a lucky charm, a reminder that we have been loved and will be loved again.

When we're alone, we can give ourselves time to create. Whether we turn to music or to art, whether we think up a perfect football play or write a poem, we can discover the person we are becoming and the one we want to be. By looking deeply into our hearts and minds, we find the inner strengths that transform loneliness into growth.

Reach Out

"To the rest of the world, we looked like the perfect family," says an adult who grew up with an alcoholic father. "No one knew, and no one in my family would talk about it. I felt so alone. . . . I don't know why I didn't scream for help."

Like this man, many of us keep our feelings to ourselves. We fear reaching out—what if no one listens? Few thoughts are scarier. A line from an old song by Simon and Garfunkel goes, "'Kathy, I'm lost,' I said, though I knew she was sleeping." Too often, we share our fears only when others cannot hear. Or we do not share them at all. This is a lonely choice, because when we do reach out, we often find we are not as alone as we thought. We see that others have the same doubts and needs as we do. Sometimes just knowing that someone cares enough to listen is all we need. At other times we need to talk to someone in particular: the parent or friend with whom we're having trouble, perhaps.

Most of us have people in our lives who can *potentially* support and comfort us. Many of us can turn to friends or parents, brothers or sisters, girlfriends or boyfriends, aunts or uncles, grandparents or teachers, coaches or clergy, our parents' friends or our friends' parents.

Trusting that someone will listen can be hard. But finding someone to talk to is worth the risk. Nothing makes us feel less lonely than being heard and understood. And we can learn to talk so that people will listen. This may seem odd, but it's true.

Here are some tips from the experts:

■ Don't try to change someone's mind. Instead, share your own feelings. You might start a talk with a parent who never listens by saying, "Will you hear me through if you know I'm not trying to change your mind?"

■ Use "I" statements instead of "you" statements. Instead of, "You make me so mad when . . .," try "I feel so angry when . . ." "I" statements don't attack the other person.

■ Make sure the other person has heard you correctly. You might even ask, "Can you tell me what you've heard so I can be sure I'm saying this clearly?" If your listener has it wrong, try again.

■ Be a good listener yourself. If you listen well, others are more likely to listen to you. Try **active listening.** Concentrate on what the other person is saying. Try not to interrupt. Repeat what you've heard to make sure you understand, even if you don't agree. We don't have to agree with one another to feel close. We just need to be heard.

None of these tips are magic. They won't instantly heal relationships. But they may open dialogue. If we talk, we may be heard. And when we are heard, we feel less lonely, even if the situation has not changed.

Another way to reach out is to follow our interests. When we do, we are more likely to find others who see the world as we do, others who may become friends.

Following new interests may mean spending less time with old friends. This isn't easy. But it is worth it if those friends no longer meet our needs. Sometimes old friends may want to join us in new pursuits. We need only ask.

Figuring out how to follow new interests isn't always easy, either. School clubs or teams and religious groups may not offer what we want. Sometimes adults can help. Melissa wanted to work with animals but didn't know how to go about it. By chance, she mentioned her interest to a teacher whose friend owns a pet-grooming store. Melissa now spends two hours a week learning to groom pets. By asking adults, "What would you do?" we can

When we give of ourselves, we feel valued and useful. We feel part of a larger community that both needs and supports us. We feel anything but lonely.

sometimes make the connections we need.

Sometimes our interests lead us to help others. We may work with the homeless or volunteer at an orphanage. We may help clean up our neighborhood or raise money to fight hunger. So much work needs to be done in the world, and every community has people who are trying. By helping them, we help ourselves. When we give of ourselves, we feel valued and useful. We feel part of a larger community that both needs and supports us. We feel anything but lonely.

Sometimes loneliness lingers despite our best efforts to get involved or to reach out to those we know. We may feel as if we will never find friendship or love. These feelings can lead to **depression.** We may feel that we'll never be happy. We may even feel that life isn't worth living. When we feel this way, we need professional help. Counselors, therapists, and some members of the clergy are trained to give that help. Seeking help when we feel troubled is not only OK—it's a strong and positive thing to do. It is a way of taking care of ourselves.

A Final Word

The loneliness we feel as teens will revisit us throughout our lives. But we have an opportunity as teenagers to learn how to deal with the feeling. If we learn to use loneliness as a tool for growth, we will be able to see it as a helpful friend rather than a frightening foe.

Loneliness can become our compass. When we are lost in the forest of our changing lives, we can use our loneliness to find a new direction. The sense of loneliness can point to relationships that need changing. It can lead us to discover new interests and talents. It can guide us in our search for who we are and who we want to be.

We cannot banish loneliness from our lives. But we can transform it. In so doing, we open the way to happiness and growth.

If You'd Like to Learn More

Books and Movies

Books and movies can help us understand our emotions better. Here are a few that deal with loneliness.

The Member of the Wedding, by Carson McCullers (New York: Bantam Books, 1978). This story by a famous writer explores the confusion and loneliness of leaving childhood behind.

Are You There God? It's Me, Margaret, by Judy Blume (New York: Bradbury Press, 1970). This is the story of Margaret, a young girl who talks to her own private God about the things that trouble her—family, friends, and growing up.

Coping with Your Emotions, by Paul J. Gelinas (New York: The Rosen Publishing Group, 1989). This book discusses the types of stress and confusion that often accompany the teenage years. The author offers advice on coping with this difficult time of life.

Go Ask Alice was written by an anonymous author (New Jersey: Prentice-Hall, 1971). This book is based on the diary of a teenage girl who becomes addicted to drugs as an escape from the real world.

Wednesday's Children (San Diego: Media Guild, 1989). This six-part series portrays teenagers dealing with peer pressure, sexual abuse, dysfunctional families, absentee parents, and loneliness.

Glossary/Index

active listening: 44 Concentrating on what someone is saying without interrupting.

alienation: 16 The feeling of not belonging.

chronic loneliness: 13 Loneliness that lasts two years or more.

community: 15 A group that gives its members a feeling of belonging.

culture: 15 The customs and beliefs that characterize a society or a part of a society.

depression: 45 An emotional state marked by feelings of sadness, despair, and discouragement.

developmental loneliness: 16 Loneliness that comes and goes during the teen years.

immune cell: 11 Cell that fights disease.

immune system: 9 The body's defense against disease.

loneliness: 6 The feeling of being cut off from important relationships.

myths: 15 Stories that capture the ideals of a society or a part of a society.

psychiatrist: 16 A medical doctor who studies how people feel, act, and think, and who treats people who are emotionally troubled.

reflective solitude: 40 Time spent alone thinking about one's life.

self-development: 32 The work each individual does to understand himself or herself and to grow psychologically.

self-sufficiency: 15 Reliance on oneself, not on others.

situational loneliness: 12 Loneliness caused by a change in one's life.

theory: 12 An unproven but well-supported idea about why something happens.

transient loneliness: 13 Loneliness that passes quickly, usually in days or weeks.